Poems Found in a Little Box in the Attic

Poems Found in a Little Box in the Attic

Poems Found in a Little Box in the Attic

53 intriguing poems

by 8 intriguing women

Christina Biel

Shirley Duncan

Faith Hudson

Anne Klump

Nancy Lang

Helen Noble

Jill Price

Emily Tye

Foreword by David Gewanter, PhD

Illustrations by Steve A. Hamdy

Edited by Anthony G. Bennett

Poems Found in a Little Box in the Attic

Library of Congress Number 2012914862
Printed in the United States of America
Printed on recycled paper.

Published by Blue Orb Books, McLean, VA
www.BlueOrbBooks.com

Foreword by David Gewanter, PhD
Illustrations by Steve A. Hamdy
Cover design by Ted C. Blair

Edited by Anthony G. Bennett

Foreword
by David Gewanter, PhD

What is the place of a poem in a life, what is its place in the world? Here are the soundings by eight women, from different cities, continents, and realms; poems spanning eighty-plus years, from the 1929 Depression and World War II to the present day. These writers have not met; they are not published, professional poets leading some literary school—and thus they need not dress their verse in scholastic uniform, nor meet the demands of an audience. "Excuse me if I don't follow your norm," confesses one poet; "There are thousands of me's / All in one body." This book brings surprises at the turn of page, and the turn of line.

Though mostly keeping to traditional rhymes and musics, the poets gathered here follow their own sudden, sometimes unexpected passions. They look away from the public world, and explore the secret details of the personal. In this realm, a girl of two is the most wondrous creation; day-lilies lean toward a fading mother; and a too-bright moon wakes up the birds. Can we trust our senses to decipher the world? All is not as it seems. To one poet, "Life is bliss in camouflage"; yet to another, the "illusions of danger" become "as real as the real ones." For these women, as for quiet rebels like Emily Dickinson, the space between people feels both intimate, and empty:

I met a friend today
Floating on the wind
A soul in a piece of dust,
From ashes.

("Dust in the Wind" by Anne Klump)

Time, too, finds its mark as each season dies into the next. The "tunnel of unbroken green" and the "brown burn burnt" of flowers tell us, "Long summer has come." Then, all too soon, the leaves fall like a "discarded summer gown." The poet's mind gathers up the past; each remembrance can pierce "the thin armour of the heart." In other moods, however, life is just for the present. A kiss breaks the boundaries; but for one sassy speaker, if a man doesn't "fit my whim," she might just "go on to other men."

To read these poets' biographies is to read of swerves and improvisation, and of the supple responsiveness of poetry to voice a life in flux: a businesswoman who winds up studying in the "School of Healing"; a biologist who visits the lost city of Petra, then suddenly writes poems; a British actress who later worked for the head Hindu Swami; a dancer who was employed at the British Signal Office, sending coded messages to the Resistance during WWII.

This last poet, Jill Price, shows a modern, contrarian spirit. Even in the teeth of war, she finds "Streams of boredom flowing on." The mix of terror and ennui, the haunting Baudelairean note, is sounded deeply in her poem, "Sunset," written in 1943:

The covering of sky is wearing thin
Through its tattered patches gleam
The livid streaks of agony
All the terrors held in dream—
The scarlet, golden, gleaming bits
Of hurt and anger pushed away
And now released through ragged splits
To squeeze the heart each close of day.

("Sunset" by Jill Price)

*

David graduated cum laude from the University of Michigan where he won the Hopwood award, and taught ESL in Barcelona before earning a PhD at the University of California, Berkeley. He is author of three books of poetry from the University of Chicago Press: *In the Belly* (1997), winner of the Zacharis First Book Prize; *The Sleep of Reason* (2003), finalist for the Laughlin Prize, Academy of American Poets, and most recently, *War Bird* (2009). He is co-editor of *Robert Lowell: Collected Poems* (FSG & Farrar, 2003), winner of the Ambassador Book Award. David has taught at Harvard and Georgetown University and lives in Washington, DC.

Poems Found in a Little Box in the Attic

Editor's Note

This book came about after I called my godmother in London to wish her a happy 90th birthday. I was telling her that I was editing my marketing textbook for the 3rd edition (I taught marketing at Georgetown University for seven years in the business school). Jill sent me 12 poems she had written over the years (including some penned during WWII) and suggested I collect some additional poems by other women and make a book of it.

I loved her poems and her idea. I have always been fond of poems as they have a rhythm and symmetry that I find soothing. I tried my hand at writing some when I was younger, apparently they weren't very good, as the young lady I was courting didn't go out with me (and I am sure that was the only reason). Perhaps at the time I just didn't understand women enough. Later I found out that listening to women and reading their works was interesting and fun. Women have a certain sensibility and civility which, in our world today, we need more of.

So, I set about seeking more poems. I called friends, relatives, and colleagues and their friends, relatives, and colleagues. A hundred phone calls later I had a trove of poems. In selecting the ones to include in this book I had one requirement: they must be intriguing, they must tell me something new and interesting. So now, I think we have a fine little book with 53 intriguing poems by eight intriguing women hailing from three continents.

I hope you enjoy the poems and perhaps you will feel inspired to write your own intriguing tale.

Anthony G. Bennett
Editor

Table of Contents

Poems Found in a Little Box in the Attic

Section One

Christina Katherine Biel

Poems Found in a Little Box in the Attic

The Tide.....by Christina Biel (2011)

The tide has turned,
But it will not do me in.
The tide has churned,
But I will not be burned.

I will admire its course
Avoiding dangers of course.
Nature is abundantly full,
Of its own push and pull.

No one can withstand her might,
So, no sense to put up a fight.
Nature inevitably gets her way,
But with strength we live through her day.

Elation.....by Christina Biel (2011)

The day grows crisp and long,
And spirits soar along,
Hopes and energy abound,
Hinting of music, but not sound.

Reason can kill,
Or at least still
The spontaneity running wild
Like an untamed child.

When things click
The clock does not tick,
Logic does not capture
The senseless sense of rapture.

Prayer for the Red Door.....by Christina Biel (2003)

With a red scarf sally,
Whither do I dally?
Serious and furious,
Sometimes so curious,
Sometimes not.
An adventure is sought.

Today is a red scarf day,
So, tell them to go away,
All little nits and gnats,
The somber gutter rats,
Those so blind not to see,
The true glory in me.

I want no hoping moping,
I want all longing gone.
Now I say, I can dance
And have a real live change
To live with some romance.

May I be over pain?
There is far more to gain.
I am in the clover,
Part of the world over,
I choose all reds for me,
Bringing beauty to see.
(cont.)

(cont.)

Red talks of no fear,
Faith is so very near,
Red is my pure color,
I know there is more,
I am wrong to think well
That I know all to tell.

Red is my symbol for passion,
More than mere fashion.
Red rings true and clear,
Perfectly strong and near,
Like the call of a French horn,
Like feeling newly born

I want to affirm, to pray.
I am blessing today,
I celebrate the life force,
Not only a matter of course.
I feel more alive, less dead,
With the pulse of burning red.

This is a new stage
At another wiser age,
I begin to hear bells ring,
A silly tune it does bring.
Life is good, life is good.
Hallelujah, from both below and above.

I will always love.

Emergency.....by Christina Biel (2011)

Emergency bells are sounding,
These impending bells are rounding,
I feel the huge chimes ringing,
Like rising voices singing.

I am ready to make huge leaps,
And I am sensing the next big bang,
Into little bits and pieces.
There is a memory of planets colliding,
And breaking apart like molecules in separation.

My reaction is to feel all my pulses in frenzy,
I look around and wonder if my inner commotion
Is showing in any external motion.
I am praying that the emergency gets a response,
And that the emergency passes.
Illusions of danger are as real as the real ones.

Comfortable Circle.....by Christina Biel (2011)

A circle starts in one place
And goes back again to the beginning.
At best, one goes at the best pace back to the best place.

So many unnecessary distractions,
Or else projections and illusions and delusions,
Can be followed as side tracks to nowhere.

Back at the beginning,
After having gone around,
The real smoothness of completion is found.

Pebbles.....by Christina Biel (2003)

An ordinary stone,
Can be given a special name.
And is no longer the same,
It is lifted from the common to the uncommon.

It is more than ordinary,
It becomes special,
Given a new name,
It resonates a sense of fame.

If a molecule acquires significance,
It is a treasure.
All and every particle is a treasure,
Waiting for its name and moment of recognition.

Small Joys.....by Christina Biel (2011)

The months creep by without a sigh,
In days of errands and sport.
Small joys are these,
Simple contentment in a simple fashion.

No grandiose schemes or strategies,
Only daily meanderings through the day.
No moments, no effigies,
Only fleeting hits of joy.

These are small crystallized moments,
There is a flash of laughter and a sense
Of devil may care,
And all is fair.

Carefree and light heartedness,
There must be something right,
A sense of play is not a plight,
A sense of play changes the day.

This gift changes speeds and changes rhythms,
Unexplainable velocities of harmony,
Where simple disharmonies yield to stronger melodies.
The gift of play is the only gift I want.

A Break up of a Relationship.....
by Christina Biel (2011)

A relationship crashed,
They parted ways.
With blame and hurt,
There are broken pieces.

Activities and stances reign,
One is alone again.
Spreading disappointment like a pool,
One or both are feeling or acting like a fool.

Feeling the pain,
Going through the stages of grief,
One by one until,
There is just weariness.

Contrary to good sense,
They knew wishful imagining or nonsense.
Both chose to follow folly foolishly.
Dejection followed self delusion.

Friends can easily say,
There will be another better day,
Another choice and another chance,
To choose another pattern and person with romance.

(cont.)

(cont.)

Forced optimism is like a scented soap.
It gives flowery hope,
And encouragement not to mope.
There will be another.

Camouflage.....by Christina Biel (2011)

Life is bliss in camouflage.
Hiding brings comfort.
Camouflage is so good,
It is understood.

Chameleons and rabbits need to be less visible,
As do soldiers in the field.
Exposure brings more risk and terror,
Being seen can be one grave error.

It takes courage to face the risk
Of being exposed.
Camouflage improves the game of hide and seek.
But, what if you want to be discovered?

Self Sabotage.....by Christina Biel (2011)

People in their perversity,
Act contrary to reason.
Funny that many take a direction,
Contrary to self protection.

Some actions seem to defy
A stated purpose and plan.
There does not seem a clear explanation why.
It is only clear that one can.

Like moths to a fire,
Seemingly mistakes are made.
Perhaps lessons will be learned,
Perhaps karmic battles will be paid.

Cats.....by Christina Biel (2011)

There was a girl named Tina,
Who had a desire to grow,
In ways that reflected her patina,
And In ways that everyone would know.

And her first step was to take in a stray cat,
Orange and mean as a wild bat,
Who would bite and bite and rally fight,
With all his rusty fury and might.

Then she took on another stray,
A little black bundle of bones,
Who had lost her little way,
And was hiding among construction stones.

New animals bring new energy into the house,
There was life and commotion under the furniture.
But it did not stay the same,
The wild cats never became tame.

They wanted out to wander,
And explore the outdoors,
And that was their end,
For they wandered off and away.

Never to return,
The wild cats returned to their ways.
She was left catless,
Waiting for the next strays.

Poems Found in a Little Box in the Attic

Section Two

Shirley Mae Duncan

Poems Found in a Little Box in the Attic

Chocolate.....by Shirley Duncan (2000)

My urge for it is diabolic
Could be I'm a choco-holic;
Melting richly on the tongue,
Pleasure secondary to none.

Chocolate sundaes, chocolate shakes,
Chocolate mousse and chocolate cakes,
Most of all I do adore
Solid chocolate, smooth and pure.

My gratitude to men unseen
For processing the cocoa bean,
Adding nuts and combinations,
Sweet delights and taste sensations.
Master-makers are the Swiss,
Moments of ecstatic bliss.

Gives me energy and vigor
(Ruining my sylph-like figure),
Can't appease or satiate
My appetite for choco-late.
Loved by millions – every race,
It makes this world a better place.

Emma.....by Shirley Duncan (1985)

Child of sunshine, hair of gold,
I watch you playing with your toys,
Feminine in all your actions,
Diff'ring so from little boys.

Carefully you dress your dress your dolly,
Daintily you tie your shoe,
Laughing, prancing, singing, dancing,
Captivating sprite are you.

Conversation so endearing,
Personality revealing,
Charm and beauty now appearing,
Unaware your heart she's stealing.

I'm her aunt. I've seen the world,
With dazzling wonders, yet it's true —
There's nowhere, nothing, quite so wondrous,
As a little girl, age two.

Retirement.....by Shirley Duncan (2005)

Both retired, we're now at leisure,
To satiate ourselves with pleasure,
Activities and friends and fun,
A golden era has begun.

The deadlines and the stress are o'er,
From great careers we had before,
We sometimes miss them but, no fuss,
We're concentrating now on US.

Two eager ships with sails unfurled,
Off we go to see the world…
Enjoy each day, for, come what may,
Time speeds by, one can't delay,
And so we fulfill each desire,
Life's special bonus, to retire.

Full Moon Rising.....by Shirley Duncan (1990)

Sphere exuberant suspended,
Silver orb of brilliance splendid,
Darkness swiftly dissipating,
Merrily the stars you're chasing,
Their flicker fades,
Before your gaze.

Superbly bright, your light tonight,
Designed to dazzle and delight,
Your special show, for us below,
We're lovers basking in the glow,
As moonbeams flow.

Such beauty stirs my soul anew,
And spirits soar on high with you,
They fly to join your joyous beaming,
Ride the silver rays now streaming,
To rendezvous,
Amid the dew.

But caution, rival of the sun,
Lest radiance reign, with nights undone,
That creatures resting, birds a-nesting,
Waken, thinking dawn has come,
And day begun.

The Bird upon My Balcony.....
by Shirley Duncan (2008)

It came as a surprise to me,
To find, upon my balcony,
Within a hanging plant concealed,
A-nesting bird; she's now revealed
Looking serious and glum,
Beside my bright geranium.
I thought from me she'd surely fly,
When we made contact eye to eye,
But there she sat complacently,
At home, upon my balcony.

She doesn't get much privacy,
(I like to use my balcony)
Some kind of dove, she seems to be,
This bird who shares her life with me.

If every time I look, she's there,
A mother with concern and care
Through wind and storm she selflessly
Protects her coming family.

How many eggs I never knew,
But now I see the babies – two,
She has a mate who pulls his weight
Providing food from morn till late.

(cont.)

(cont.)

They'll soon be gone, as life moves on,
I'll miss the active company
But maybe next year, hopefully,
Again they'll choose my balcony.

Expectation.....by Shirley Duncan (1983)

Baby dear, you'll soon be here
Can hardly wait till you appear
Into a world which, as you'll see
Is quite a splendid place to be …
With twinkling stars and golden sun,
Laughter, ice cream, toys, and fun.

You hover on the brink, apart,
Safely hiding, time abiding,
Beneath a mother's beating heart –
Your lullaby, as warm you lie,
Perhaps reluctant to depart.

Till comes that magic day – the dawn,
When you'll be born.

The dance of life begins with pain,
Thereafter, joy can surely reign –
A world of wonders to explore
Outside your door,
A bond of love which could endure
For evermore.

You'll join the ever-flowing stream –
A tiny traveler, yet unseen,
May destiny, salubriously
Fulfill your every hope and dream.

Parade of the Tall Ships.....by Shirley Duncan (July 4, 1992)

Five hundred years this nation grew
Beginning fourteen ninety-two,
A celebration grand this day
In New York harbor, calm and grey.

Through morning mist which never clears
Ghostly white, a ship appears;
Soaring masts with sails outspread,
A splendid cavalcade she led.

From many lands and climes they hail,
Thirty ships, all under sail
Gliding gracefully in line
Echoes of a bygone time…

Centuries of explorations,
Empire-building, new-found nations,
Brave Magellan, Captain Cook,
Living pictures from a book.

The Mayflower and the Bounty bold,
The Pinta, ships with tales untold,
In replica so very small
But in achievement, giants all.

(cont.)

(cont.)

Phantom travelers in the gloom,
Welcomed by the cannon's boom,
Colored flags and pendants fly,
History parading by
The tow'ring skyline of New York:
Columbus – what would he have thought?

Words.....by Shirley Duncan (2002)

Friendships, living — day to day,
Much depends on what we say
And we are judged, for wrong or right
By words we say and words we write.

Words determine how we feel
Words can hurt then words can heal
Words inspiring, words to sing,
Words abusive, words which sting,

Words of wisdom, kindness, care,
Happy chatter children share,
Words we cherish, love's expression,
Words of comfort ease depression.

Words of hope in dark distress
Words which set the mind at rest,
Pleading words we can't ignore,
Words to make the spirits soar.

Words on using, words absurd
Words we wish we hadn't heard,
Words we say and then regret,
Words we know we'll not forget.

(cont.)

(cont.)

Even words when we're alone,
Spoken on the telephone.
Conversation was binding ties
Weave the fabric of our lives.

Often times, we win or lose
By how we choose the words to use,
They may mislead, insinuate,
Angry words can devastate.

Nor do words of condemnation
Often help the situation.
Criticism, words which scold,
Suddenly one's world grows cold.

For though your thoughts be not unkind,
Alas, we cannot read your mind,
We've only heard
Your spoken word.
And words, like thoughts, fly on the wind,
And once released do not rescind.

Poems Found in a Little Box in the Attic

Section Three

Elisabeth Faith Hudson

Poems Found in a Little Box in the Attic

O Memory.....by Faith Hudson (1954)

O Memory, from whom I sought to flee,
To hide from every image of the past.
'Twere better find eternal peace in thee,
Than from my tortured inner self be cast.
The gurgling water, muddy and distraught,
The faded mansions of another age
Watching the world go by – the world I ought
To know: the hungry souls, black bars, iron cage.
I hear the traffic with its ugly roar,
The click of heels, the sounds that never cease
To conjure up grim fears of death and war
And ghosts of those I loved in days of peace.
Thus do I find I cannot close the door.
O Memory, I'll fly from thee no more.

Poems Found in a Little Box in the Attic

Section Four

Anne Marie Klump

Poems Found in a Little Box in the Attic

Windy Day.....by Anne Klump (1986)

A sudden gust,
A rushing breeze,
Blowing every one and thing
Molding my clothes against my body,
As if I wasn't wearing any at all
Exposing every line and curve
Yet whipping me into anonymity
So no one knows who goes there
To whom does that body belong?
A silky mass of hair
Obscuring all facial features
A cloud of gold
Mystery and anonymity
Gone in a breeze
A chance lost.

Ignore Them......by Anne Klump (1990)

Ignore them
It isn't time
Don't waste these intense feelings
On someone you don't love,
Someone who does not love you.
Wait.

But, what if the time does not come
What if love never comes
Loneliness remains
And props his feet up on my coffee table,
And stays
The hole in my heart remains.

Some people like being alone always
Not me.
I feel I need a significant other,
A soul mate,
Someone to love
Someone who loves me
Where is he?
Is he?

Pardon Me, But I Beg to Differ.....
by Anne Klump (1986)

Pardon me, but I beg to differ
I can't just follow the crowd
I have to be me
Even if it is lonely.

Excuse me if I don't follow your norm
But to me that would be false.
The quote, "Be true to thy self"
Was meant to be lived, not put on a shelf.

It's the odd character
That gets the attention
And makes us laugh
Because she dares to be different.

Doing things that are different,
And often times rare,
Breaking a stereotype,
Escaping a snare.

Being unique is like going
The wrong way down a one-way street
Be different if you dare
Live life without a care!

(cont.)

(cont.)

Fashions are different
Or you can invent your own, for
If we all dressed and acted alike,
Life would be boring, I'd go insane.

Life is to be lived,
And enjoyed as you wish
Choose your own path,
Your individuality cherish.

The Dreamer.....by Anne Klump (1994)

Looking up
I see the soles of your feet
As you hang on to a cloud
Peering over

The Dreamer
With your head in the clouds
Your dreams have no limits
Other people's reality is just a word to you.
It hits you and bounces off
Making no dent in your shell
As you smile and turn around
Looking at the next dream.

Ideas jumping in your head like lightning
Sparking your excitement.
Your enthusiasm is unstoppable
As your mind races forward
Then you rush on,
In pursuit of your next dream.

I see your toes,
As you tip toe up
Peering over the next cloud.
Hopefully someday,
Your dreams will become
A reality.

A New Spring.....by Anne Klump (1986)

You were a leaf
pressed between the pages
of my life

I am the Autumn
I added color to your life
and you to mine

Now is the time
to fall away

And alight anew
while I grow colder

In hopes
of a new Spring.

Who am I.....by Anne Klump (1986)

Who am I and who are you?
Is there any reason why we met?
Do we know each other from the past
Or in the future?
Or are you just a filler in my life,
With no real meaning or lasting slot...?
Only time will tell.

Who am I
I cannot tell you
I do not know
I can't see me
We are one
And can't see me objectively
I can't get far enough away to look
Not even a millimeter of space
Between me and I.

(cont.)

(cont.)

Everyone has different views and opinions
Even if I told you who I was
You may not agree,
Life is subjective.
You cannot see through my eyes,
Nor I through yours.
So you see, I am not one person,
But thousands...

The many people that others see
Each with their own views of me
I am all views
There are thousands of me's
All in one body
"Where do you hide them all,
You haven't gained an inch."

Center.....by Anne Klump (1986)

Self centered
Whirlpool
Vortex
Spiral shell
Sun
Dot
.

There is a center,
But is there an edge?

Dust in the Wind.....by Anne Klump (1986)

I met a friend today
Floating on the wind
A soul in a piece of dust,
From ashes.
The wisdom and compassion
I gained from that micro dot...
A picture is worth a thousand words.
I felt of eternity
Gained years of experience
Floating in the wind.

Priam's Kingdom.....by Anne Klump (1983)

Is love at first sight possible?
Or feasible at all?
I'm usually quite logical,
But now I am up against a wall.

Every time he is near,
His eyes through me sear.
And mine like magnets draw
To that face without a flaw.

As strongly as this disturbs me
He still seems quite impervious
When he gets too near I flee
Alas, my feelings must be obvious.

If I could by chance meet him,
I'd either remain quite smitten,
Or decide he does not fit my whim,
And go on to other men.

But first I must discover,
A coy and normal meeting,
So I won't have to hover,
In this middle footing.

(Priam was the King of Troy)

Poems Found in a Little Box in the Attic

Section Five

Nancy Lang

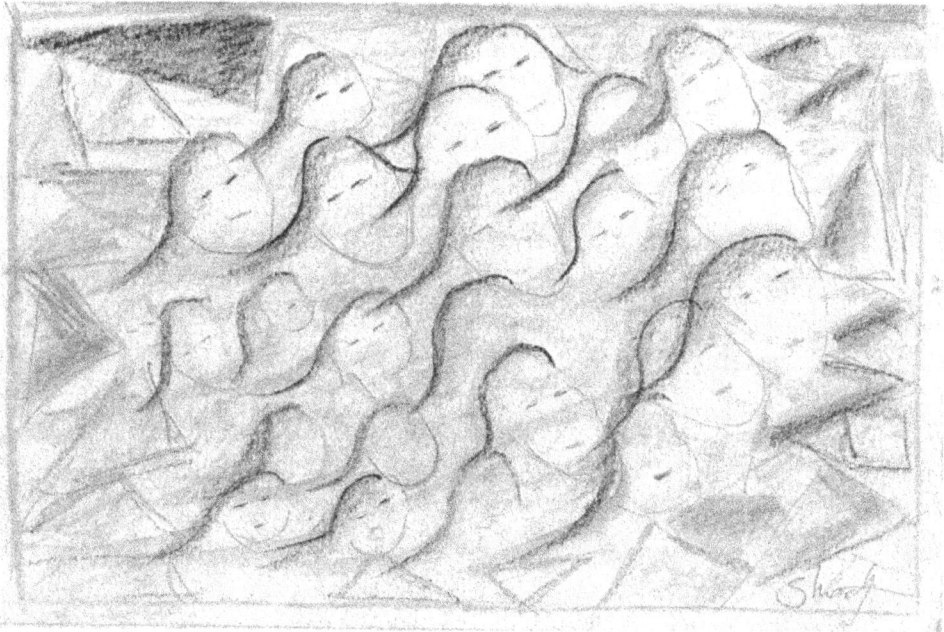

Poems Found in a Little Box in the Attic

My Heart is Beating.....by Nancy Lang (2001)

My heart is beating
It's my inner soul churning
Ecstatic for
A new found love.

From where did it come
This urgent desire
That now
Awakens in me?

I sigh, I touch,
We kiss, we embrace.
The boundaries are gone
Yet a pulsing remains.

Save It for Another Day.....by Nancy Lang (2004)

The sun is falling
Come
Catch it
Hang on to
Its numinous rays
Less endless nights
Hold sway.

Watch – I need to
Cling to those beaming rays
Though clouds might
Obscure the way.

Flay them away
Make the sheen
Bright light
Stay.

Out of the foiled darkness
Keep it safe
Let it rest
Save it
For another day.

Charisma.....by Nancy Lang (2005)

I sought the word
But did not know how to spell it
I searched in Webster
But the letters did not fit.

I knew it began with a "C"
But the rest seemed a travesty.
Perhaps Roget would set me straight
Here I'd find its matching duplicate.

But my synonym search failed to work
The missing word would not convert.
Not with words such as attraction,
Charm, or magnetic action.

I wanted this to end
So I called a friend.
Simple "h" was really all that I sought
But not knowing: where is the thought!

Another solution I also discovered
My computer has words that spelling errors can recover
But still it is true: you must know how to spell the word.

What We Don't See.....by Nancy Lang (2005)

We fail to witness those souls forgotten
Lamed by fate and prejudices be gotten;
We fail to see
How their tragic life has gotten.

Though hopeless and downtrodden
Because their communal help is rotten,
We fail to see
For our humanism misbegotten.

A Way to Happiness.....by Nancy Lang (2003)

A caterpillar and a golf tee met one day in June.
The grass was green, the flowers were in bloom.
Said the caterpillar to the tee:
"Be careful. People will swing at you and me."

Said the golf tee to the caterpillar:
"Indeed, this game is a thriller;
And soon you will change
And fly away to another range."

"Yes" replied the worm, "my change will be soon
When I shall disappear into my cocoon.
And you dear tee, what will become of you?
Will you be left butchered, broken in two?"

"Oh Mr. Caterpillar" replied the tee incensed,
We've got a purpose that makes much sense –
You as a butterfly and me as a stick –
We'll make people happy – and that's the trick."

Oh Socrates.....by Nancy Lang (2007)

Who am I? What do I want?
>> To be focused
>> To control time
>> To be engulfed with love
>> To do it all
>> And to joyfully live.

Extraneous diversions bombard me
Divert me from my inner pole
Enticements with subterfuging strokes
Throw subtle ego indulgences
Destroying the centered balance

>> Like pleasing people
>> Or striving for monetary easiness
>> Or seeking mental achievements

And what will I have left behind
When I have finished all that I could be?

Orfeo you certainly wouldn't miss me.

(Monteverdi's *Orfeo* is credited as the first opera.)

Silent Strings Still Sing.....by Nancy Lang (2005)

Sounds of music endlessly floating
If out to the portless sea:

Do you remember the silent harmony,
The humming of my eternal tune
The soundless melody
Re-echoing all I play.

A silence,
A pause;
Then, a continuing grand pause ---
And everlasting ethereal quietness.

Tell me: What thoughts, what songs,
What fragment sounds rebound?
Are you listening to the sounds within
To the endless harmony of my tones?

Gone may be my voice,
My melodic vocal outpourings
My tears of mystic laughter
Hidden in eternity's beating of time
Yet my silent strings we'll always sing.

Poems Found in a Little Box in the Attic

Section Six

Helen Marie Noble

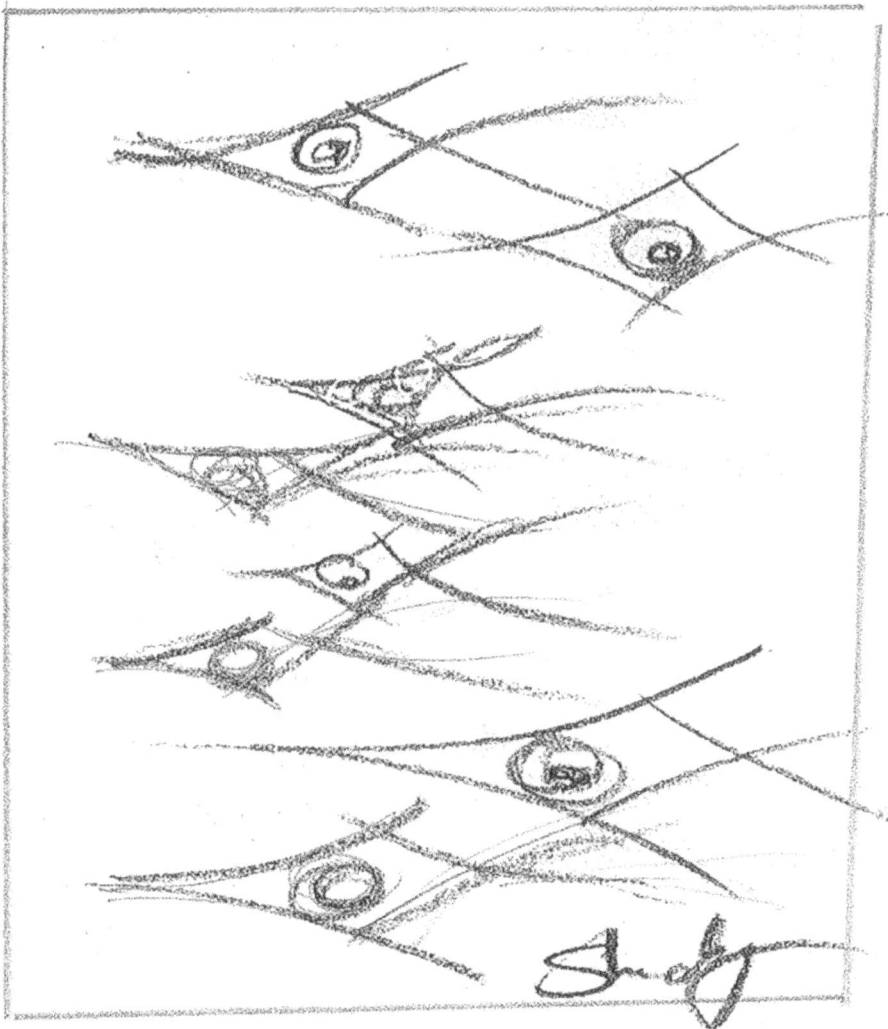

Poems Found in a Little Box in the Attic

Taxpayer's Lament.....by Helen Noble (circa 1947)

What's happening to our world today?
Can we go on living this crazy way?
What future is there in life for me
In this world of today, where nothing's free?
It's tax for this and tax for that,
If anything's free, I'll eat my hat;
And I've been told that some folks say,
The air we breathe will be taxed some day.
We used to do our work each day,
At the end of the week, we drew our pay;
Now before we get it the Government's there,
To take out what they call their share.
Some younger folk who know no better,
Will think an old crank wrote this letter;
But, heck, all that I'm trying to say,
Is, "How did it ever get this way?"
We had a war some years ago,
But isn't it time, I'd like to know,
That tired old taxpayers like me,
Got some of our Government's charity?
When I think of all the money I've made,
And the dollars in taxes I've paid and paid,
And see that things aren't one bit better,
I felt inclined to write this letter.
Now I love my country, don't get me wrong,
And I want to see it get along;
But please, "Uncle Sam," won't you think of me,
When you're giving my dollars away for free?

Evelyn, Dorothy and Helen.....by Helen Noble (1929)

Three little girls with curly hair,
Evelyn, large and tall,
Dorothy, with writing talents,
And she is very small,
Helen, quick tempered and nervous,
She tries to cure this trait,
Each willing to do her service
Form morning till very late.
Dorothy is still a student,
Arithmetic is her despair,
She really tries to study hard
For she knows that her sisters care,
If her marks are better than usual,
Of praises she gets aplenty,
But if her marks are unusually low,
She knows she'll not get any.
Evelyn works for a living
Is employed by the N.E.A.
That she earns every cent of her salary
"Yes" we can truthfully say,
For two years she's worked and earned money,
And board she has faithfully paid,
And out of those two years' earnings,
A nice lump of money she's saved.

(cont.)

(cont.)

Helen, a creature of impulse,
At insurance has worked two years long,
And though she's earned just as much money,
Has not even saved a song,
Spend thrifty and always buying
Some silly knick-knacks and then,
Gives them away or throws them away,
And starts right in spending again.

Poems Found in a Little Box in the Attic

Section Seven

Muriel Jill Price

Poems Found in a Little Box in the Attic

The Statue.....by Jill Price (1943)

Moulded of common clay by life's rough hands,
An image of proportions tall and slim –
Varnished a gleaming whole by Death's quick stroke –
Shines far around, though tears may sometimes dim.

Not now for him the slow decay of time,
Worries and ills that chip away the mould
And leave of Life's best work but few remains –
The stony fragments of each one gone cold.

But he shall stay, whole Life was quick and bright.
Rising above the ruin all around.
His radiance now may help to light our paths
Which lead the way he has already found.

Remembrance.....by Jill Price (1942)

Memory was once a pleasant thing
A cosy blanket to be drawn around
On winter evenings, bring joy
And a sense of peace that lingered.

Now it is no longer so
Each remembrance is an arrow
Piercing the thin armour of the heart,
Letting in the bitterness of loss
To flood the mind with answerless despair.

But I will weave a new design
From threads of present doings and desires.
Calm pool of Life unrippled by deep feeling
You shall make a smooth, unbroken surface
To mirror future contemplation.

Sunset.....by Jill Price (1943)

The covering of sky is wearing thin
Through its tattered patches gleam
The livid streaks of agony
All the terrors held in dream —
The scarlet, golden, gleaming bits
Of hurt and anger pushed away
And now released through ragged splits
To squeeze the heart each close of day.

Autumn Afternoon.....by Jill Price (1943)

Drifting, dry autumnal leaves
Like discarded summer gown,
Float from the trees they once adorned
Now greens have burnt to browns.

Their crinkled outlines blur the path
Are trampled by foot and wheel.
Thus are the lives so lightly tossed
Of those who could think and feel.

Easter in Devon.....by Jill Price (1938)

Recorded beauty, cataloging its delights –
The sudden sweep of hills,
Smudge of heather-coloured shadows.
Thatched, white washed farm
Pictured in perfect perspective.
Scurrying streams, amber, clear,
Too turbulent for reflection –
This is true beauty,
But my unleaping heart is waiting
And my eyes, lead lidded like a thundery day
Close themselves without emotion.

(County of Devon, England)

Lament.....by Jill Price (1950)

O how I wish that Life could be
Like the film, where all we see
Are movements of intensity.

And all the boring bits between,
Like tidying up and making clean
Pass unrecorded, seldom seen.

Chestnut Trees.....by Jill Price (1951)

Tender buds, virgin tipped
Burst from sticky cases
To become Christmas tree candles
Lightly spaced.

Chrystal edges blur
Over blossomed boughs
Scattering snow-flake pieces
Softly down.

Tree touches partner
Forms a tunnel of unbroken green.
Stark candles brown burn burnt –
Long summer has come.

Signal Office, Grendon Underwood.....
by Jill Price (1944)

Streams of boredom flowing on
Endlessly on, to what eternal sea?
A sea of tears shed as each Soul finds out –
This is all that life will ever be.

(WWII Special Operations Executive signal office in
Grendon Underwood in the County of Buckinghamshire,
England)

Artist Unknown.....by Jill Price (1937)

Who has drawn the winter trees?
Etched clear against the darkling sky?
Quick scribbled symmetry of twigs —
I know I could not even try.

Did they shape the outline first?
Ink-brown lines against the blue.
Which tea-time turns to milky pink —
I'm quite sure I could not — could you?

Who would have the time to spare?
For blocking in each separate line
And working out the infinite shapes —
I only know the task's not mine.

Stay In Touch.....by Jill Price (1998)

Brr — brr — brr — brr
Hello, this is the Go, Go, Go Travel Co.

For destinations in the sun
Please press button No. 1.
If Russia is the place for you
Employ button No. 2.
When you wish to pay a fee
Use the button No. 3.
Should you want to book a tour
You must press button No. 4.

I want to know the price of a flight to New York
Please, oh please start to talk.

For destinations in the sun
Please press button No. 1.
If Russia is the place for you
Employ button No. 2.
When you wish to pay a fee
Use the button No. 3.
Should you want to book a tour
You must press button No. 4.

To book a ticket to New York
It really would be good to talk.

Springtime.....by Jill Price (1980)

In the spring a young man's fancy
Lightly turns to roadside holes.
All these pipes that need replacing,
Let's get digging like the moles.

Never tell the utility services
Where your latest work's begun
They might think that they could share it
And that would really spoil the fun!

(With apologies to Alfred, Lord Tennyson.)

Summer is a comin'.....by Jill Price (2004)

Summer is a comin' in
Smells of barbeque
Buyeth meat for charcoal heat,
And light the barbeque
You've invited WHO?

Children rush about and squealeth,
Mothers pick them up and healeth
Neighbours turneth
Fathers burneth
Vive le barbeque, beque, beque.

Well done cooking barby-wise
Now we'll drink the apple-tise.

Section Eight

Emily Tye

Poems Found in a Little Box in the Attic

Looking Glass.....by Emily Tye (2011)

Looking out the glass door on the
Last day in June I see my mother.
She is sitting in the hammock-chair
With her back to me but turns when she hears me open the
door.
I yelled at her about something that wasn't her fault
Just because I could.
She looked at me without saying much,
Blinking apologetically.
Her eyes look big and round behind her thick glasses.
When I go back inside she turns around and bows her head
back over her book,
Feet crossed like a child.
Over by the pond all the Day Lilies lean toward her,
Straining across the lawn to touch her,
Like orange trumpets with their faces open.
She's their mother too,
All the flowers in the garden bloom in gratitude.

Summer in Charleston.....by Emily Tye (2011)

Big yellow house on the corner
Of Comming and Morris with
The dark brown window panes
Behind the Monarch
Development sign next to the
Empty lot with the patches
Of grass between the rubble…
There are books piled up
And boxes next to a lamp on the
Second story,
Below it girls dance in the
Kitchen, backlit
Like shadows in the yellow light
Their hands lifted up as if
Around an altar.
I can see the music in their
Movement but I don't hear a thing.
Naked silence.

Biographies

Authors

Christina Katherine Biel

Ms. Biel, born in Paris France of a European mother and an American father, has lived in France, Switzerland, Germany, and in the east coast, west coast, and in the southern US. Raised in a military family, Ms. Biel had the chance to move often and developed an appreciation for travel, international perspectives, and the great diversity of the human experience. Her education and interests are varied, reflecting an open mindedness, curiosity, and generous spirit. Ms. Biel received a BA in art history from Bryn Mawr, followed by an MBA in finance from The George Washington University. Her work experience has been consistently in telecom, domestically and internationally, most recently in support of the federal government. Her motivation is to live fully, both spiritually and physically. Ms. Biel has pursued both business courses and a wide range of energy healing courses, including completing a four year certification at the Barbara Brennan School of Healing. She keeps active physically by running (completed two marathons) and yoga. Also, since she can remember, her musings, dreams, ideas, experiences, and insights have all been collected in her journal, some thankfully taking the form of poetry. Now, having been in the work force for more than 25 years, Ms. Biel aspires to keep her sense of humor and lightness and bring it to others, simply and lyrically. Ms. Biel now lives in McLean, VA.

Shirley Mae Duncan

Ms. Duncan was born in Melbourne, Australia. She studied Biology at Melbourne University, after which she worked for a year as a hospital laboratory technician. Ms. Duncan then set off to bicycle around Australia with a girlfriend and a dog, the trip took over a year and is described in Ms. Duncan's book *Two Wheels to Adventure*. Ms. Duncan then came to America with a contract for lecture-tours, and for 10 years she lectured to schools and dinner clubs all over the U.S. speaking about her Australian trip and her further worldwide travels. "I never thought that I could write poetry," she said, "until I was inspired by a visit to Petra, the fascinating 'lost city' in Jordan. The words came easily and writing the poem was fun, like a game with words. I really like the challenge of 'finding the rhyme'." She has loved poetry since school days, especially the poets Wordsworth and Tennyson. Ms. Duncan is now working on her collection of travel poems about her favorite places and far flung adventures. She lives in Washington, DC.

Elisabeth Faith Hudson

Ms. Hudson was born in Norfolk, England in 1927, and grew up there on her father's farm. Ms. Hudson graduated from the Royal Academy of Dramatic Arts in London. After graduation Ms. Hudson joined an acting troupe that performed in England and France. Later Ms. Hudson became the aide to the head Hindu Swami in England for seven years. Ms. Hudson was fond of tennis, lacrosse, skiing, and won several sailing competitions. Ms. Hudson's first introduction to poetry was a poetry book given to her as a gift by her father's military secretary during WWII. Ms. Hudson passed away in 2001.

Anne Marie Klump

Ms. Klump was born in Winter Haven, Florida. She lived there for only four years before moving with her family to Austin, Texas. She has been an artist since age four, when her mother, who was also an artist used to bring paints to the beach every summer and encourage all of her four children to paint. Ms. Klump was the only one who really took to art. She graduated from The University of Texas with a major in Architectural Studies and a minor in Graphic Design. In college she was on the rowing team and played volleyball. She loves to travel to other countries, meet people, try the many culinary delights, and wander through art museums and beautiful old churches. And so, after college, she travelled to Europe several times as well as Australia, New Zealand, and the Caribbean. Her latest and happiest career is that of an Interior Designer and Faux Painter and Muralist. She has owned her own company for 15 years. Ms. Klump enjoys snow skiing, hiking, volleyball, and swimming, as well as reading and writing poetry. While she likes many poets, two of her favorites are Robert Frost and Lord Byron. She collected several handwritten books of poems others have written. She said she started writing poems because as a young woman, she was very passionate, felt things deeply and needed to express these feelings trying to figure things out and see if anyone else could relate.

Nancy Lang

Ms. Lang was born in New York City and grew up on Long Island where she began studying the violin at age six. She received a Bachelor of Music at Skidmore College and went on to get an MA in music from Columbia University. Ms. Lang taught grade school music on Long Island, and handled all the string programs and conducted two orchestras and an operetta. Next came fourteen years in New York City; first at WQXR, the Radio Station of the New York Times, then at WTFM, the first Stereo station in the New York area, as the station music director. Following that she did some national radio syndicated music programs with Alfred Wildenstein and Igor Kinas. In 1965 she went to Washington, DC to work at the Voice of America as a Music Specialist. Ms. Lang wrote scripts on American musical events, conveying America's cultural aspects that were broadcast overseas by our 49 different language services at the VOA, for 27 years before retiring in 1994. A musical highlight was being the first woman to conduct the National Symphony in Washington, DC. It was a family program event, where she conducted Handel's "Water Music Suite". Paul Hume (the harsh Washington Post music critic for 35 years who gave President Harry Truman's daughter Margaret a bad review for her concert) gave Ms. Lang a good review. Ms. Lang currently lives in McLean, Virginia, performs the violin in the McLean Symphony, reviews operas for an Austrian magazine, and has been President of the American News Women's Club and President of the Women's Club of McLean. Ms. Lang started writing poetry early in life as she wrote her own Christmas cards as poems that captured her life's activities for that year.

Helen Marie Noble

Ms. Noble was born in 1915 and lived with her mother and sisters, Evelyn and Dorothy, in Washington, D.C. most of her life. When her mother passed away in 1930, the sisters lived together. Ms. Noble began writing poetry as a teenager. Later, she typed out her poems and pasted them into a blank book. Ms. Noble worked for decades at People's Life Insurance Company in Washington D.C. (in the building that is now the Saudi Arabian embassy). Ms. Noble passed away in 1986.

Muriel Jill Price

Ms. Price was born and raised in London, England. After high school she went to dance school and became quite skilled. Ms. Price was teaching dance when WWII broke out. She was asked to join the Special Operations Executive (SOE) where she was a wireless operator sending and receiving coded messages to and from the Resistance movements in France, Holland, and Norway. After the war, Ms. Price taught dance for over 40 years ultimately at her own dance studio. Currently, she remains in London where she teaches English as a second language to immigrants in London and continues with her hobby of painting water colors. Ms. Price can't remember specifically when she first became interested in poems as she feels she has always had an interest since childhood. Ms. Price passed away in 2012.

Emily Margaret Tye

Ms. Tye was born in 1988 in Fairfax, Virginia. She graduated from the College of Charleston in South Carolina, majored in Classics and minored in English. While Emily was in college she studied abroad in Florence, Italy and worked as a tour guide at the Duomo Cathedral (part of a UNESCO World Heritage Site). Ms. Tye has been a substitute teacher in Fairfax, Virginia and is currently assistant director of media and events coordination for A.R.T. & Associates. She will be attending Kings College London in the fall of 2012 for a graduate degree in Classical Art and Archaeology. Emily has been writing for as long as she can remember. It is the tool by which she interprets the world, her observations and her emotions.

Illustrations

Steve A. Hamdy

Mr. Hamdy was born and raised in Alexandria, Egypt. Growing up he played soccer and volleyball and traveled to and worked in fourteen countries in Europe, Africa, and Asia. He received his Bachelors degree in Accounting from Alexandria University. Mr. Hamdy then moved to the United States when he was 22. He initially took up art as a hobby, was self-taught, and is now adept in pencil, acrylic, and oil, and works as a freelance artist in his spare time. Mr. Hamdy owns and manages a restaurant in McLean, Virginia where he lives with his wife and two children.

Editor

Anthony Gordon Bennett

Mr. Bennett received his BBA and MBA from The George Washington University. He worked for AT&T and Union Camp, was a Special Assistant in the George H. W. Bush Administration, taught as an adjunct lecturer of Marketing for seven years at Georgetown University, and lobbied Congress on behalf of the Solar Energy Industries Association. He is now President of Blue Orb Tunes and Blue Orb Books. He lives in McLean, Virginia and has twin sons.

Poems Found in a Little Box in the Attic